Bible Stories

Selected for 3-4 year olds

Retold by
Kathleen Crawford

Illustrated by Roma Bishop

ABINGDON PRESS
Nashville

Preface

There are ten stories in this selection, specially chosen for children aged 3-4.

In *The baby in the basket* we see that God can protect us and care for us.

In *Elijah, the good man* we see that God can provide us with all we need.

The story of the lost sheep reminds us that God knows and loves each one of us.

Each one of these stories shows us something of what God is like.

Contents

1. God makes our world 4
2. The baby in the basket 8
3. David fights the giant 12
4. Elijah, the good man 16
5. Jesus, the baby King 20
6. The story of the lost sheep 24
7. The four friends 28
8. The runaway son 32
9. The man in the tree 36
10. Jesus is alive! 40

God makes our world

In the beginning, everywhere was dark. The world had no shape at all. A strong wind blew across the water that covered all the earth.

And God said, "Let there be light."
God made light and darkness, day and night. God made the sky, land and seas. And God saw that all these things were good.

Then God said, "Let trees and plants grow on the earth." And fruits, and vegetables, and beautiful flowers, and trees of all kinds began to grow.

God made the sun, moon, and stars to shine in the sky.

And God saw that all these things were good.

God made fish and all kinds of interesting creatures to live in the sea and many different birds to fly in the sky. God made lots of different kinds of animals to live on the land.

And God saw that all these things were good.

Then God made people to take care of the new, beautiful world.

"My world is here for you to use and enjoy," God said.

And God saw that all these things were very, very good.

The baby in the basket

God's people, the Israelites, had been living in Egypt for some time. But now there was a new king. He did not like the Israelite people. He made them work very hard. And he decided that there should be no more baby boys.

One day, an Israelite woman had a new baby son. His family loved him very much. But they knew that if the Egyptian soldiers saw him, they would take him away. So they kept him hidden at home.

When he was tiny, the baby slept most of the time, but as he got bigger, he made more noise.

His mother was frightened. "We must find somewhere safe to hide him," she said to her daughter, Miriam.

They both looked around them. They looked at the River Nile which was close by. Then God gave them an idea.

The mother wove a basket, rather like a cradle, and made it waterproof on the outside. She lined it with soft blankets. Then she gently put the baby inside and hid the basket among the tall rushes growing by the river.

"Stay nearby and keep watch," she told Miriam.

That afternoon, the princess of Egypt came to swim in the river. Suddenly she heard a noise.

"What's that?" she asked her maid. "It sounds like a baby crying."

The maid discovered the basket.

"What a beautiful baby," smiled the princess. "I'll call him Moses. He can live with me at the palace."

Miriam thought quickly. She ran out from her hiding place and curtsied to the princess.

"Would you like someone to help you look after him?" she asked.

"Yes, please," replied the princess.

Miriam ran home and fetched her mother, who was very happy to work for the princess. She knew Moses would be safe now, and she could still look after him. And when Moses grew up, he became a very important leader of God's people.

David fights the giant

David was a shepherd boy. He looked after his sheep well. Sometimes he saved them from lions and bears.

One day, David went to see his brothers who were soldiers in the Israelite army. They were fighting the Philistines. On the other side of the valley there was a great, tall man walking up and down. He was the Philistines' best soldier.

"That's Goliath," said David's brothers. "He wants someone to fight him. Whoever wins the fight, wins the battle."

"Who will fight him?" asked David.

"We're all too frightened," said the Israelites. "Just look at him!"

"I'll go," replied David.

"You?" they said. "But you're not a soldier."

The soldiers took David to see the king.

"You'll need some armor," said King Saul. "Borrow mine."

David put on the helmet. Too big. He tried to lift the sword and shield. Too heavy. He put on the suit of armor. No good.

David took his shepherd's sling. Then he chose five smooth stones from the stream. He was ready to meet Goliath.

"Is this a joke?" laughed the giant.

"God will protect me," David told him.

The giant laughed all the more.

"Who is your god?" he sneered.

Then David put one of the stones in his sling and hurled it at Goliath. It hit him on the forehead and Goliath fell down dead.

All the Philistines ran away. All the Israelites cheered loudly. God had won the battle for them.

"You see," said David. "God looked after me."

Elijah, the good man

In the land of Israel there was a bad king called Ahab. He did not care about God. He did not care about doing good.

There was one good man who pleased God. He was called Elijah. One day Elijah went to see the king with a message from God.

"There will be no more rain in this land until you say 'sorry' for the bad things you have done, and learn to do good things," he said.

King Ahab was furious. Elijah was frightened. Elijah went to hide near a clear stream so that he had water to drink. Then God sent ravens to bring him food. Before long the stream dried up. There was hardly any food in the land.

"What do I do now?" Elijah said.

"I'll look after you," God promised. And he told Elijah where he could go to find food.

Elijah walked to a village. There he saw a woman gathering firewood.

"Please would you give me something to eat?" he asked.

"I'm sorry," answered the woman, "but I only have enough flour and oil for one small loaf for my son and me. Then I shall have nothing left."

"First make a small loaf for me," said Elijah. "Then make another one for you and your son. God has promised that you will have enough."

The woman did what Elijah told her. Every time she used some flour, the jar filled up again. Every time she used some oil, the bottle filled up again. God made sure that they all had enough to eat.

Jesus, the baby King

As the donkey trotted slowly along the road to Bethlehem, Mary knew that her baby would soon be born. "Could we stay here, please?" Joseph asked at each place they came to. But there was no room for them anywhere.

One innkeeper saw how tired Mary was.

"You could stay in the stable, if you like," he said. "It's warm and dry in there."

That night Jesus was born. Mary used the animals' manger for his cradle.

Up in the hills near Bethlehem some shepherds were looking after their sheep. It was a cold, dark night. Suddenly, there was a very bright light and the shepherds heard singing. The sky was full of angels.

"Don't be frightened," the angels told them. "We've come with good news. Today, God's son has been born in Bethlehem."

The shepherds rushed down the hillside and went to see the new baby.

Many miles away in another country, some wise men had seen a bright star.

"It means a royal baby has been born," they said. "We must go and see him."

They followed the star a long way until they found the place where Jesus was.

They gave him three very special presents
– gold, frankincense and myrrh.
  And Mary, Jesus' mother, thought
about these visitors, the shepherds and
the wise men. She knew Jesus was a very
special baby.

The story of the lost sheep

Jesus was good at telling stories. One day he told the people about a sheep which got lost.

"It was getting dark and it was almost night-time.

"'Time to bring the sheep into the fold,' thought the shepherd.

"He had one hundred sheep and he knew them all. The shepherd led them down the rocky path, guiding them with his crook.

"As the sheep went into the fold, the shepherd began to count them: one, two, three, four, five... all the way up to ninety-nine.

"'Oh dear,' he said. 'Perhaps I've made a mistake.'

"He counted them again. It was not easy because they were all moving around. One, two, three, four, five... all the way up to ninety-nine. One sheep was missing.

"'I must go and look for it,' said the shepherd. 'It might be hurt.'

"So the shepherd walked back up the hill, looking everywhere as he went. He searched for a very long time.

"At last, he heard a faint bleating. The sheep was caught in some thorn bushes. It was struggling to get free. The shepherd gently lifted the exhausted sheep on to his shoulders and carried it back to the fold.

"And this time when he counted his sheep, he counted one, two, three, four, five... all the way up to one hundred.

"God is like that shepherd," said Jesus at the end of the story. "God can't be happy until each of us is safe."

The four friends

There was once a man who couldn't move his arms or legs. He spent each day lying on his mattress watching people go by. One day, four of his friends arrived.

"Come on!" they said. "We're going to see Jesus. We've heard he can make sick people well."

"But I can't go," the man said. "I can't move my arms or legs."

"We'll carry you," said his friends. They each took one corner of his mattress and carried him carefully to the house where Jesus was.

Jesus was talking to people about God. There were crowds and crowds of people there. The four friends tried to get through the door, but there were too many people. There was no way they could take their friend to Jesus.

Then they had an idea. They went up on to the flat roof of the house and carefully made a hole in it. They lowered their friend down into the house – right in front of Jesus.

Jesus looked at the man. "Stand up and walk," he said.

The man could feel his hands and toes tingling. He could move his arms and legs!

He stood up, just as Jesus had told him. Everyone was amazed!

His friends watched what was happening and smiled. They knew that Jesus could make their friend well again.

"Thank you!" they said.

The man rolled up his mattress and tucked it under his arm. Then the five friends walked off happily together.

The runaway son

Jesus once told a story about a farmer who had two sons.

The younger son said to his father, "When you die, will your money be shared between me and my brother?"

His father nodded. "Well," continued the younger son, "could I have my share now?"

"All right," his father said. He was sad because he loved his son. He knew he would get into trouble.

The younger son took the money and left home. He travelled to exciting places, ate delicious food, had parties and made many new friends. He bought presents for his friends and expensive clothes for himself.

He was very happy.

But soon the money had all gone. And then his friends didn't want to know him any more. In the end he got a job feeding pigs. Sometimes, he was so hungry that he ate some of the pigs' food. It tasted horrible! He was very unhappy.

At last he decided to go back home. "I'll ask if I can work as a servant there," he said. "I don't deserve to be treated as a son. But at least I'll get enough to eat."

As the son walked towards home, his father saw him and ran out to meet him.

"I'm sorry I was so selfish," said the son. "Can I be a servant in your house?"

But his father gave him an enormous hug.

"I've been waiting for you to return," said the father. "Let's have a party and celebrate! Welcome home, son."

Then Jesus said, "God is just like this. However bad we've been, God never stops loving us."

The man in the tree

Nobody liked Zacchaeus. He was a rich man and he was a cheat. His job was collecting taxes and he always collected too much and kept some money for himself. Nobody wanted to be his friend.

One day, Zacchaeus heard that Jesus was coming to his town. He had heard about Jesus. He talked to people about God, and told them how much God loved them.

In the town there were crowds of people everywhere. Zacchaeus stood on tiptoe, but he was not very tall. He could not see anything. He tried to wriggle through to the front row, but people pushed him back.

"Go away, you horrible man," they said.

Zacchaeus felt sad. He really wanted to see Jesus.

Then he had an idea. He climbed up a tree and hid among the leaves. He had the best view of all and no one could see him. As Jesus came along the road, everyone cheered loudly. Suddenly he stopped beneath the tree where Zacchaeus was hiding.

"Zacchaeus," said Jesus, "please climb down. I'd like to come to your house for a meal."

The crowd gasped. Why did Jesus want to eat a meal with someone like Zacchaeus?

"He's a bad man, that Zacchaeus," they grumbled.

Zacchaeus and Jesus talked for a long time and they became friends. Zacchaeus was sorry that he had cheated people. He promised to give them all their money back – and some extra as well.

After Jesus became his friend, Zacchaeus was never the same again.

Jesus is alive!

Mary was so sad. Her friend Jesus had died and she would never see him again.

Very early in the morning, just as the sun was beginning to rise, Mary and two other women set off for the tomb where Jesus had been buried. It was inside a cave and the entrance had been closed by a huge, heavy stone.

When they got there, they saw that the heavy stone had been rolled to one side. They looked inside the tomb. Jesus' body had gone!

Suddenly they saw two angels sitting near the tomb.

"Are you looking for Jesus?" they asked.

"Yes," answered Mary.

"He isn't here any more," the angels told her. "He is alive."

Mary could not believe it. She sat outside the cave, crying. Then she saw a man she thought was the gardener.

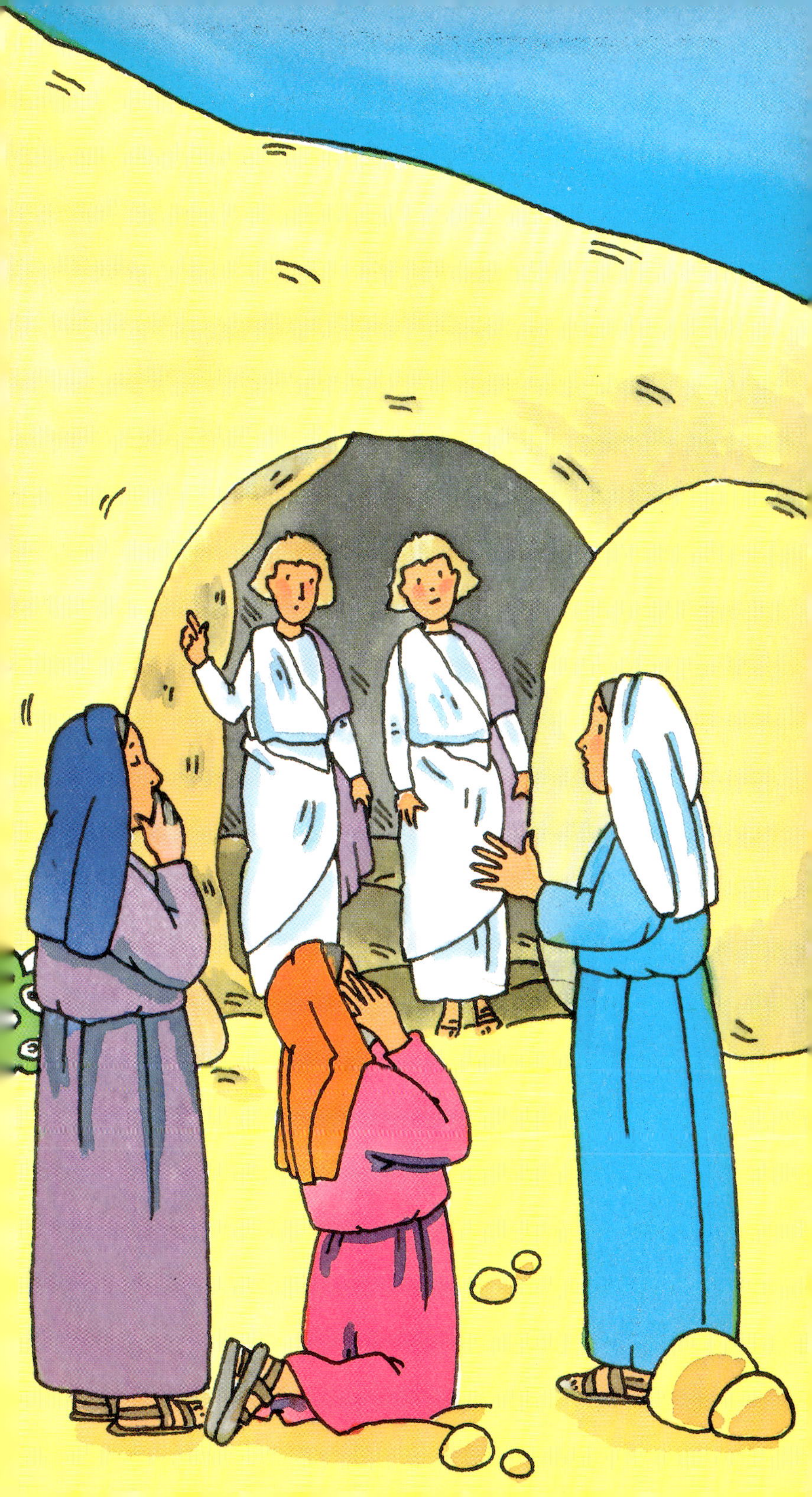

"Do you know what has happened to Jesus?" she asked. "Has someone moved his body?"

"Mary," the man said softly.

Then she knew that he was not the gardener at all. Mary knew his voice. It was Jesus! He really was alive!

Mary rushed to tell everyone the good news.

"Jesus is alive!" she shouted. "Jesus is alive!"